The Lady of Shalott

Alfred Tennyson

A Victorian ballad

"The Lady of Shalott" is a Victorian ballad by the English poet Alfred, Lord Tennyson (1809–1892). Like his other early poems – "Sir Lancelot and Queen Guinevere" and "Galahad" – the poem recasts Arthurian subject matter loosely based on medieval sources. Tennyson wrote two versions of the poem, one published in 1833, of twenty stanzas, the other in 1842 of nineteen stanzas.

The poem was loosely based on the Arthurian legend of Elaine of Astolat, as recounted in a thirteenth-century Italian novella titled Donna di Scalotta (No. LXXXII in the collection Cento Novelle Antiche), with the earlier version being closer to the source material than the later. Tennyson focused on the Lady's "isolation in the tower and her decision to participate in the living world, two subjects not even mentioned in Donna di Scalotta."

Alfred, Lord Tennyson

Alfred Tennyson, 1st Baron Tennyson (6 August 1809 – 6 October 1892) was Poet Laureate of Great Britain and Ireland during much of Queen Victoria's reign and remains one of the most popular British poets.

Tennyson excelled at penning short lyrics, such as "Break, Break, Break", "The Charge of the Light Brigade", "Tears, Idle Tears" and "Crossing the Bar". Much of his verse was based on classical mythological themes, such as Ulysses, although In Memoriam A.H.H. was written to commemorate his best friend Arthur Hallam, a fellow poet and fellow student at Trinity College, Cambridge, who was engaged to Tennyson's sister, but died from a brain haemorrhage before they could marry. Tennyson also wrote some notable blank verse including Idylls of the King, "Ulysses", and "Tithonus". During his career, Tennyson attempted drama, but his plays enjoyed little success. A number of phrases from Tennyson's work have become commonplaces of the English language, including "Nature, red in tooth and claw", "'Tis better to have loved and lost / Than never to have loved at all", "Theirs not to reason why, / Theirs but to do and die", "My strength is as the strength of ten, / Because my heart is pure", "To strive, to seek, to find, and not to yield", "Knowledge comes, but Wisdom lingers", and "The old order changeth, yielding place to new". He is the ninth most frequently quoted writer in The Oxford Dictionary of Quotations.

The Lady of Shalott

Part I

On either side the river lie

Long fields of barley and of rye,

That clothe the wold and meet the sky;

And thro' the field the road runs by

   To many-tower'd Camelot;

And up and down the people go,

Gazing where the lilies blow

Round an island there below,

   The island of Shalott.

Willows whiten, aspens quiver,

Little breezes dusk and shiver

Thro' the wave that runs for ever

By the island in the river

   Flowing down to Camelot.

Four grey walls, and four grey towers,

Overlook a space of flowers,

And the silent isle imbowers

   The Lady of Shalott.

By the margin, willow-veil'd,

Slide the heavy barges trail'd

By slow horses; and unhail'd

The shallop flitteth silken-sail'd

   Skimming down to Camelot:

But who hath seen her wave her hand?

Or at the casement seen her stand?

Or is she known in all the land,

   The Lady of Shalott?

Only reapers, reaping early

In among the beared barley,

Hear a song that echoes cheerly

From the river winding clearly,

   Down to tower'd Camelot:

And by the moon the reaper weary,

Piling sheaves in uplands airy,

Listening, whispers, "'Tis the fairy

   Lady of Shalott."

Part II

There she weaves by night and day

A magic web with colours gay.

She has heard a whisper say,

A curse is on her if she stay

   To look down to Camelot.

She knows not what the curse may be,

And so she weaveth steadily,

And little other care heat she,

   The Lady of Shalott.

And moving thro' a mirror clear

That hangs before her all the year,

Shadows of the world appear.

There she sees the highway near

   Winding down to Camelot.

There the river eddy whirls,

And there the surly village-churls,

And the red cloaks of market girls,

   Pass onward from Shalott.

Sometimes a troop of damsels glad,

An abbott on an ambling pad,

Sometimes a curly shepherd-lad,

Or long-hair'd page in crimson clad,

   Goes by to tower'd Camelot;

And sometimes thro' the mirror blue

The knights come riding two and two:

She hath no loyal Knight and true,

   The Lady of Shalott.

But in her web she still delights

To weave the mirror's magic sights,

For often thro' the silent nights

A funeral, with plumes and lights

   And music, went to Camelot:

Or when the Moon was overhead,

Came two young lovers lately wed;

"I am half sick of shadows," said

   The Lady of Shalott.

"I am half-sick of shadows," said the Lady of Shalott
by John William Waterhouse, 1916

Part III

A bow-shot from her bower-eaves,

He rode between the barley sheaves,

The sun came dazzling thro' the leaves

And flamed upon the brazen greaves

   Of bold Sir Lancelot.

A red-cross knight for ever kneel'd

To a lady in his shield,

That sparkled on the yellow field,

   Beside remote Shalott.

The gemmy bridle glitter'd free,

Like to some branch of stars we see

Hung in the golden Galaxy.

The bridle bells rang merrily

   As he rode down to Camelot:

And from his blazon'd baldric slung

A mighty silver bugle hung,

And as he rode his armour rung,

   Beside remote Shalott.

All in the blue unclouded weather

Thick-jewell'd shone the saddle-leather,

The helmet and the helmet-feather

Burn'd like one burning flame together,

    As he rode down to Camelot.

As often thro' the purple night,

Below the starry clusters bright,

Some bearded meteor, trailing light,

    Moves over still Shalott.

His broad clear brow in sunlight glow'd;

On burnish'd hooves his war-horse trode;

From underneath his helmet flow'd

His coal-black curls as on he rode,

    As he rode down to Camelot.

From the bank and from the river

He flash'd into the crystal mirror,

"Tirra lirra," by the river

    Sang Sir Lancelot.

She left the web, she left the loom,

She made three paces thro' the room,

She saw the water-lily bloom,

She saw the helmet and the plume,

    She look'd down to Camelot.

Out flew the web and floated wide;

The mirror crack'd from side to side;

"The curse is come upon me," cried

    The Lady of Shalott.

The Lady of Shalott looking at Lancelot
by John William Waterhouse, 1894

Part IV

In the stormy east-wind straining,

The pale yellow woods were waning,

The broad stream in his banks complaining,

Heavily the low sky raining

  Over tower'd Camelot;

Down she came and found a boat

Beneath a willow left afloat,

And round about the prow she wrote

  The Lady of Shalott.

The Lady of Shallot by John William Waterhouse, 1888

And down the river's dim expanse —

Like some bold seer in a trance,

Seeing all his own mischance —

With a glassy countenance

   Did she look to Camelot.

And at the closing of the day

She loosed the chain, and down she lay;

The broad stream bore her far away,

   The Lady of Shalott.

Lying, robed in snowy white

That loosely flew to left and right —

The leaves upon her falling light —

Thro' the noises of the night

   She floated down to Camelot:

And as the boat-head wound along

The willowy hills and fields among,

They heard her singing her last song,

   The Lady of Shalott.

Heard a carol, mournful, holy,

Chanted loudly, chanted lowly,

Till her blood was frozen slowly,

And her eyes were darkened wholly,

    Turn'd to tower'd Camelot.

For ere she reach'd upon the tide

The first house by the water-side,

Singing in her song she died,

    The Lady of Shalott.

Under tower and balcony,

By garden-wall and gallery,

A gleaming shape she floated by,

Dead-pale between the houses high,

    Silent into Camelot.

Out upon the wharfs they came,

Knight and burgher, lord and dame,

And round the prow they read her name,

    The Lady of Shalott.

Who is this? and what is here?

And in the lighted palace near

Died the sound of royal cheer;

And they cross'd themselves for fear,

   All the knights at Camelot:

But Lancelot mused a little space;

He said, "She has a lovely face;

God in his mercy lend her grace,

   The Lady of Shalott."

Printed in Dunstable, United Kingdom